CHANGING CAREER SUCCESSFULLY

Tips for taking your career
in a new direction

Written by Renée Francis
Translated by Emma Hanna

Coaching 50MINUTES.com

WHAT IS THE SECRET TO CHANGING CAREER SUCCESSFULLY?

- **Problem:** what steps do you need to take in order to ensure a stress-free career change?
- **Uses:** successful attempts to change career can help you to thrive both professionally and personally. First, you need to take some time to reflect in order to figure out what drives you, what job you should aim for, which training is best suited to your needs, and so on. This approach will help you to achieve your new goal.
- **Context:** personal development, career management, professional wellbeing.
- **FAQs:**
  - How should I choose my new job?
  - Am I too old to change career?
  - Are some jobs more suited to a career change than others?
  - I am not satisfied with my current job, but I

have a permanent contract. Is it wise to give it all up?
- How can I support myself financially during a career change?
- What pitfalls should be avoided?

In this day and age, it is very rare for employees to keep the same job in the same company throughout their entire career. Routine, dissatisfaction, excessive pressure, and a desire for change are just a few of the motives that lead people to change careers, and it is of course essential to make a decision this important for the right reasons. Perhaps you have already been thinking of finding a new job, but have been overwhelmed with doubts at every critical juncture. Maybe you are worried that you may have difficulty finding a new job or that you would not enjoy a different profession; maybe you are unsure what training you will need, or how you will support yourself financially. All of these questions can lead to stress and frustration, but do not worry: although any change involves an element of risk, this risk can be calculated and anticipated, which will help you to avoid a royal disaster. In some ways, changing career is about knowing when to slow things down, so take the time to read through our advice and take a step-by-step approach to your new career plan. In just 50 minutes, this book will help you to change direction without losing your way.

A STRESS-FREE CAREER CHANGE: THE BASICS

A search for meaning

The main driving force behind career changes is a search for meaning. Finding a purpose in our daily lives is a quintessentially human concern, and with good reason, given that working is no longer just a way of earning a living, but also contributes significantly to our overall wellbeing. During the course of our career, we may find that the passion that used to drive us has waned, or that our values no longer align with those of the company we work for and its culture. This can lead to a lack of motivation and ambition, and frustration with the tasks we are given. At its core, a search for meaning is about feeling valued, believing that your work is worthwhile, and feeling useful.

Any search for meaning will inevitably come with

periods of doubt. However, re-evaluating your situation is the only way you will be able to find meaning in your professional life and put your own wellbeing first. As such, you should never approach a career change without first engaging in a period of meaningful reflection and intros-pection. Ask yourself the following questions:

- What aspects of my job are most important to me? Is it interpersonal interaction, income, intellectual stimulation...?
- Do I need a job that aligns with my personal values?
- Do I need recognition and validation?
- What is my greatest ambition in life?

Your answers to these questions will give you food for thought. For example, if you consider interpersonal interaction to be the most impor-tant aspect of your job, then you should maybe consider leaving your career in accountancy for a job in communication or another social-ly-oriented field.

Changing career for the right reasons

As time goes by and we gain more experience,

our goals tend to shift. People in all kinds of circumstances – from those who are just embarking on their career or who are returning from maternity leave to those who have just been fired or promoted – find themselves longing to change career. However, before you set out in a new direction ask yourself what drew you to your current position and how you ended up in it. Did you choose your profession or did it choose you? Were you able to complete your studies? Would you have liked to go into another field? Is your job related to your training? These questions will help you to identify anything that may have gone wrong along the way.

If you feel like your current position does not quite suit you, a career change could be the solution. Even if you tried to fulfil your dreams in the past and failed, there is nothing stopping you from being successful if you try again. However, always be careful when interpreting these signs, as it is possible that this period of doubt will only be fleeting. In that case, changing career for the wrong reasons would be a mistake, and may not bring you the happiness you seek. Before making a decision, it is crucial to analyse your motivations for wanting to change career in order to ensure that they are well-founded and that you are not acting on the spur of the moment. Try filling out the table below to get a clearer picture of what is driving you towards a potential career change.

Motivation	Yes	No	Order of importance on a scale of 1 to 5	Comments
Desire for fulfilment				
Sector				
Colleagues				
Family				
Partner				
Income				
Schedule				
Age				
Challenges				
Stress				
Burnout				
Develop a talent				
Boredom				
Ambition/ dream				
Health				
Other				

© 50MINUTES.com

Next, ask yourself what the real driving force behind this desire for change is, underlying all of the other motivations you have mentioned (both those you ticked and those you added to the table above). Humans have a real knack for coming up with excuses, especially when we have to justify ourselves. However, it is imperative that you identify the real reason driving you, as this will remain constant. The other reasons or justifications motivating your career change are just dressing – though that does not take away from the fact that they do have their own role to play, as they will tip the balance one way or another when the time comes to make your final decision. Nonetheless, it is best to focus on your main motivation so as not to get distracted, as this will allow you to approach your career change more calmly. If you have several strong reasons, be careful with the following ones, as they tend to be transitory:

- the atmosphere at your job has become unbearable;
- you are having difficulties with your colleagues;
- you are not entirely sure what you want;
- you have a need for constant novelty;
- you are unsatisfied with your salary or your duties, etc.;
- your close friends are pushing you into changing career for any reason;
- etc.

In fact, nothing is set in stone in the professional world, and it is entirely possible that in six months' time, the manager will have changed, or you will be promoted, or that difficult project will be shelved, or the friction between you and your colleagues will have been smoothed over, and so on. If you are feeling nothing more than general discontentment, take a few days off to give yourself some space and clear your head. However, if your potential career change is motivated by a real goal that you have been thinking about for some time, then it is worth giving it a shot.

Research the job market

Before taking the plunge, analyse the balance of supply and demand on the job market to avoid taking unnecessary risks. Gather all the relevant information: where are the gaps in the market? What is the competition like? Do you have a specific skill or a solution that corresponds to a particular need? Take a look at the job postings in the sector that interests you, ask around in your network, and take a quick look at the range of financial prospects. This will unearth new leads for you to follow and help you to avoid the riskiest propositions.

FINDING THE RIGHT PATH

After working in the same sector for several years, it can often be difficult to step into another. Some people already have their entire career mapped out, but for others, the future is still hazy. There is no magic formula that will help you to work out your ideal career; however, self-analysis is often the best solution for those who are still searching for it. Keep your mind open to possibilities and opportunities during this exercise – massive doubts can often lead to the most startling epiphanies.

Defining your needs

Abraham Maslow's (American psychologist, 1908-1970) hierarchy of needs, generally represented as a pyramid, outlines five groups of fundamental needs:

Maslow's hierarchy of needs

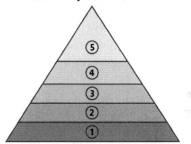

(1) **Physiological needs**
(breathing, eating, drinking, sleeping, etc.)

(2) **Safety needs**
(safe environment, stability, survival, etc.)

(3) **Belonging/love needs**
(communicating with others, belonging
to a group, etc.)

(4) **Esteem needs**
(feeling appreciated, useful, valued, etc.)

(5) **Self-actualisation needs**
(personal development, fulfilment, etc.)

Start by considering your basic needs before
moving on to the higher levels of the pyramid.
Naturally, it is more important for your future job
to ensure your survival than to meet your need
for recognition! In order to accurately assess

your needs, make sure to distinguish between your needs, desires and skills. For example, just because you want to become a comic book illustrator, it does not mean that you will be any good at drawing. Alternatively, these kinds of skills are sometimes more of a hobby than a real passion. Desires are born of choice, not necessity, so it is important to be sure of what is really essential for you so that you can find a truly meaningful, fulfilling career.

Take your desires into account

While taking your needs into account is an absolutely fundamental part of any successful career change, do not overlook your desires entirely or you risk tiring of your new job very quickly. If you do not have a career plan and you are finding it difficult to figure out what you want, start by making a list of all the aspects of your job that you dislike most: finishing at 9pm every evening, moving around, and so on. Once you have drawn up this list, it will be easier to figure out what you want. If you have a specific goal which is motivating your career change, then part of your path will already be mapped out for you. However, it is still worth considering your goals and desires in more depth so that you can draw up a more specific plan for your career change.

In any case, always be cautious: being highly motivated is great, but it can cut both ways. Do not automatically assume that all of your hopes and dreams will come true – becoming an astronaut is a wonderful dream, but achieving it is not within everyone's reach. On the other hand, do not give up at the first hurdle. Make a list of the pros and cons of your goal and see which way the scales tip.

> "I have always wanted to travel. My dream job was to become a wildlife journalist. I am absolutely fascinated by documentaries about the wildlife living on the massive nature reserves in Africa. However, that job will never be more than a dream for me. My passion for nature and animals will never be as important to me as my family and my attachment to my home. Furthermore, even if I took photography classes, I would never be able to earn a high enough income, so it was easy for me to make my choice." (Xavier)

"My son has gone into catering at markets and events. Riding high on his successful experiences working in restaurants and for a well-reputed catering service, he decided to launch his own business in response to the growing public demand for food trucks. It is an innovative formula, and for the moment it is enjoying considerable success. It is really a partial career change, given that he already worked in this sector. However, it is a totally different approach compared to anything he was used to. Before getting started, he had analysed all of the details objectively: client demand, his own desire for self-employment, and his skills to see the project through. His working hours are fairly restrictive, but no more so than when he worked in a restaurant. What has changed, however, is how much he has been thriving since he started this new job." (Johanna)

BE POSITIVE!

Changing career can often be a stressful experience. To combat this, try incorporating some self-validation into your mindset. Do not be too hard on yourself, as this can lead to frustration and dead ends. On the contrary, encourage yourself and tell yourself that you are going to succeed. You will be more likely to get a professional foothold with an optimistic attitude, as future recruiters or partners will be more likely to perceive you as inflexible and dissatisfied if you adopt a pessimistic attitude.

Émile Coué (French psychologist, 1857-1926), one of the forerunners of positive thinking, maintained that autosuggestion conditions an individual to create their own wellbeing, with the reverse being equally true – if you envision yourself falling off a ladder, it will make you more anxious and increase the risk of failure. Major athletes also use this positive conditioning technique, particularly through visualisation. If you imagine yourself securing your ideal job, you will gain confidence and motivation.

Draw up a professional and personal overview

To achieve your goals, you need to know your own strengths and weaknesses. The best way of figuring them out is to draw up a professional and personal overview, as a summary of your experiences and skills gives you an excellent foundation to base your career change on. Be pragmatic so that you can identify your stren- gths and weaknesses realistically. Use your CV to help you with your self-analysis, making sure to cover all of the following points for each of the positions you have held in the past:

- sector;
- role(s);
- acquired skills;
- duration;
- reason(s) for leaving;
- a source of professional satisfaction or a pro- fessional challenge you overcame – how did you overcome this challenge, and what skill tipped the balance in your favour?;
- any other important notes about your position;
- what you liked about the position and why.

Depending on the way you approach this exer- cise, it can give you a general overview of your- self, or a detailed map of your personality, needs, desires, strengths and weaknesses. It gives you the chance to take a step back and keep things in perspective, no matter what choices you are facing. It may also lead you to identify a common thread (which may be professional, personal, moral or intellectual in nature) linking your past experiences, which will then guide you through your career change.

> "I have always had a real passion for fashion, especially for accessories. After working as a consultant in a firm for several years, I gave birth to my first child. For me, that was the catalyst – during my maternity leave, I realised that I felt unfulfilled by my work. When I looked over my CV with an analytical eye, I realised that I had market analysis skills and a talent for presenting my ideas effectively. This was the push I needed to embark on a career creating fashion accessories. Since I was already accustomed to working with clients, I quickly made essential contacts which allowed me to develop and promote a line of accessories. I work just as much as I did before, but the difference is that I no longer see my work as a chore. My passion for fashion and my analytical mind were my guiding stars." (Olivia)

A successful career change involves a certain amount of personal doubt. Be careful with this – it is not a question of changing everything about yourself, but rather, of learning how to better understand yourself so that you can find the job that suits you best. Answer these two questions:

• How would you describe yourself in five words?

- How would your close friends describe you in five words?

Our inner being does not always correspond exactly to the self-image we project externally. Although other people's perceptions of you are not as important as the way you perceive yourself, they can nonetheless prove useful, as they offer you an alternative perspective and may allow you to identify aspects of your personality which could prove useful or problematic.

AN EXTERNAL PERSPECTIVE

Do not hesitate to ask your close friends for advice about what field or job they think would suit you. Be careful – that does not necessarily mean that you should follow their advice to the letter. Simply take the points that seem important on board. Although it can be helpful to listen to a variety of opinions, do not forget to take a step back and think about it yourself, as you will be the one who has to get up and go to work every morning! That means that the final decision is also entirely in your hands.

In order to get to know yourself better, try getting in contact with a professional coach, or make use of a psychological evaluation tool like the MBTI (Myers-Briggs Type Indicator). This personality test, which was developed by Katherine Cook Briggs (psychological theorist, 1875-1968) and her daughter Isabel Briggs Myers (psychological theorist, 1897-1980), determines an individual's personality type based on their reactions and behaviour. However, some caution is advisable, as the test is not 100% reliable and should only be used for guidance, so approach it with a critical mindset. Do not heedlessly throw yourself into applying for a four-year degree in law just because the test claims that you would make an excellent lawyer – you need to take your own skills and desires into account too.

THE IDEAL JOB

During the process of changing career, do not forget to enjoy yourself. Part of the reason why you are making this change is so that you can put your own wellbeing first and make the most of your life. Think about your dream job: opening your own club, owning a private island, teaching yoga, or working as the vet at a zoo – let your imagination and creativity run wild. Maybe you will never actually make a go of that ideal job, but this exercise may lead to ideas about similar jobs that you would be more suited to.

Analyse your plans

Once you have mapped out your ideal career, it is time to come back down to earth, because you will need to consider things from a pragmatic standpoint if your career change is to be a success. One tool which is particularly popular in marketing but which can be applied equally well here is the SWOT matrix, which gives an overview of the Strengths, Weaknesses, Opportunities and Threats of a project, concept or product. Use the following diagram to sum up the most important aspects of your professional prospects:

The SWOT matrix

Internal

STRENGTHS
What are your skills
and abilities?
What sets you apart
from the competi-
tion?

WEAKNESSES
What are your weak
points?
Will your plan be
expensive?
Will it be difficult to
build customer
loyalty?

Positive

Negative

OPPORTUNITIES
What are the
emerging fields
and markets?
Is there a
particular
demand?

THREATS
What are the poten-
tial external obsta-
cles you could come
up against?
Are new competitors
arriving on the
market?

External

© 50MINUTES.com

Use the information outlined in your SWOT
diagram to adapt your plans according to the
supply, demand, opportunities and threats you
have identified.

Be innovative

No matter whether your career change involves moving to a different department of the same company or launching your own business, you need a starting point. But just because you need a clean slate does not mean that you should simply wipe it clean and start drawing the same picture from scratch – take a new approach entirely, think outside the box, and be innovative. Every career change needs at least a speck of creativity to give you a fresh mindset.

Innovation can come in many forms and at different scales – it can mean anything from taking on a new role to launching a new project. Staying in your comfort zone can limit your potential and your ambitions; the key to a successful career change often lies in considering new ideas or ways of approaching your work. For example, if you are a property manager and are thinking of moving into improving late-night parking availability for locals in urban areas, why not get in contact with local businesses and collaborate on the development of a mobile app to manage available spaces?

The key to being innovative and creative is to identify the needs around you, or your own needs. There is no need for mental gymnastics; simple, effective concepts generally make the best ideas. By imagining it, you will already be sketching out a plan for your career change – a much more effective approach than stumbling around blindly.

Lifelong learning

If you decide to go into a radically different field in which you do not have extensive training, you will doubtlessly need to widen your knowledge base or study for additional qualifications. Even if you stay in the same sector, do not rule out the possibility of taking additional or higher training to develop new skills. Investigate the possibilities available to you at universities, colleges, or in social programmes, employment agencies, recruitment offices, professional associations, and so on.

Continuing your studies is a choice which, as well as providing you with new training, is sure to benefit you by inspiring you and helping you to forge new connections which will be helpful as you move forward. However, if you intend to continue your studies or take additional training, your career change will take longer. This is something you should take into account with regard to your financial situation, and means that there will be two choices available to you:

- If your financial situation is stable enough or if you are able to secure financial aid (grants, loans, etc.), you can of course quit your current job in order to fully commit yourself to your new project. Make sure that you are well informed about your options before handing in your notice, as they will vary by country: you may be able to take a sabbatical leave, individual training leave, entrepreneurial leave, or another similar option.
- If your resources are more limited, you can ask your employer if you can switch to a part-time contract, or try to find evening or correspondence courses.

EMPLOYMENT STATUS

Your new career path may also lead to a change in your employment status (employee, employer, self-employed, etc.). This can be a big change to get used to, especially if you are intending to become self-employed, as it takes a great deal of planning. There are countless administrative, financial and legal hurdles to overcome, and the regulations are constantly changing. Consult someone who is an expert on the subject: the human resources department, a tax expert, notary, accountant or lawyer, for example. Consultations can sometimes be expensive, but having all the information you need at hand will help you to avoid any nasty surprises.

Bouncing back after a failure

Another key to a successful career change lies in knowing how to bounce back. If your plans fall through, consider it a valuable professional experience and figure out what you can learn from it. A failure can become a springboard or an unexpected stepping stone that leads towards a new goal. Try to identify the underlying reasons for each failure:

- Were your objectives poorly defined?

- Were you just unlucky or were you badly prepared?
- Does the job really suit you?
- Were you forced to give up due to a lack of financial resources?
- What additional steps could you have taken to ensure your success?

Depending on your answers to these questions, either rectify the flaws in your strategy and continue in the same sector you were initially targeting or readjust your aims. If you are still in the research phase, do not hesitate to rethink things. Most importantly, do not lose confidence in yourself if you do not succeed on the first try, and do not lose faith in your entire plan; simply adjust the weaker aspects of it.

TOP TIPS

- **Stay mentally young and dynamic.** There is no age limit for career changes; it is an option for anyone who has the determination to forge a new path. If you have a few extra years under your belt, your professional and personal experience will weigh in your favour and will give you a strong base to help you succeed as you embark on a new chapter.

- **If you do not have much experience, ask someone older than you for advice.** Since you cannot bank on your experience during a job interview or a meeting, use your personality and your individual strengths. Highlight the things that make you unique so that you stand out.

- **Use networking and make your list of contacts your greatest ally.** If you do not yet have any useful contacts to help you develop your idea or project, do not underestimate the importance of networks and modern communication tools. Join seminars, discussion groups and social networks such as LinkedIn,

Viadeo, Facebook, and so on. Start by targeting the people who would make the most useful contacts, and remember to continually manage your network, as these contacts could easily become future clients or ambassadors for your product or service. Good communication is half the work!

- **Before jumping into a project, analyse the costs.** Drawing up a business plan is an essential step which will not only help you to visualise the structure of your project, but will also shed light on the costs and schedule necessary to carry it out. Furthermore, if you are moving into a career in business, market research will also be essential. Finally, make sure that you are adequately informed about any administrative processes or bank dealings you will have to handle.
- **Find the rhythm that suits you.** If your main goal for your career change is to take your foot off the pedal, opt for a part-time job or a position with fewer responsibilities. However, adjusting to a new rhythm is not always a simple matter. If you are the kind of person who finds it difficult to slow down, find a balance between maintaining your professional

vigour and learning to take a step back.

- **Do not rush into things;** it will only lead to failure. You need to take time to reflect and to work through your thoughts in order to make the correct decision that will lead to a successful career change. If you need to undergo additional training, you will also need a great deal of patience. Again, do not rush this process: wait until you are ready and have the cards stacked in your favour before you throw yourself in at the deep end.

- **Look into evening or correspondence courses.** This will allow you to keep your current job during the process of changing career, which can make things easier at an organisational or financial level.

- **Be realistic.** Before changing career, make sure that your dreams are not straying too far from reality. Just because you are looking for a new job, it does not mean that your quality of life is going to change dramatically. Be enthusiastic without being naïve, as setting your expectations too high can only lead to disappointment. Keep your feet firmly on the ground and learn about the job market and the training available to you before you start, while also considering all the various aspects of the new area you are hoping to enter in advance. If you decide to make a career change based on the assumption that your future job will bring you total fulfilment, you may be trying to flee from a problem that cannot be solved by simply changing career. Any job, whether as an employee or an employer, comes with a whole host of obligations and limits.

- **Write your plan out and set deadlines for yourself.** Even though it can take a lot of time and effort to prepare, a schedule will help you to stay on course and to readjust your goals, if necessary.

FAQS

HOW SHOULD I CHOOSE MY NEW JOB?

Do not take this step lightly. For some people, the sector or job they want to pursue is a foregone conclusion, but for others, it is less clear and can only be determined through a process of inner reflection. Drawing up a personal and professional overview will help you to create a list of your strengths and weaknesses, skills and aspirations, and will therefore help you to choose a fulfilling job. Before taking the plunge, make sure that you are aware of the current economic climate by researching the job market.

AM I TOO OLD TO CHANGE CAREER?

No generation has a monopoly on career changes. However, your age can help you decide which of your strengths to emphasise. For example, a 40-year-old employee will have a certain level of experience, and will be able to contribute that experience to a project and ensure that old mistakes are not repeated, whereas someone with less experience could bring their creativity, fresh perspective and ability to adapt quickly to the table. Every age bracket has its own advantages.

ARE SOME JOBS MORE SUITED TO A CAREER CHANGE THAN OTHERS?

Depending on the job market and the jobs available, yes. Certain sectors are more saturated than others, but there is nothing to stop you from trying your luck, so long as you are adequately prepared and motivated. This is why it is so important to carry out thorough market research before you make your move.

I AM NOT SATISFIED WITH MY CURRENT JOB, BUT I HAVE A PERMANENT CONTRACT. IS IT WISE TO GIVE IT ALL UP?

Ask yourself the right questions before you take the plunge. Why are you not satisfied with your job? Is it because of the work atmosphere or because of your responsibilities? Are you bored? Analyse your answers to make sure that you are contemplating a career change for the right reasons, and do not quit your job unless you know what you will do afterwards. Take time to think things over, as a permanent contract is certainly something that should be taken into account. Depending on the means at your disposal (support from your family or your spouse), consider whether or not you have the necessary resources to support yourself in the immediate future after quitting your stable position. One of the key aspects of any career change is being organised enough to manage the change without falling into difficulties. Drawing up a plan and setting objectives can greatly help you through your career change, even if you initially hold on to your permanent contract.

HOW CAN I SUPPORT MYSELF FINANCIALLY DURING A CAREER CHANGE?

There is no magic formula; there are so many specific cases that it is impossible to sketch out a general road map. However, there are a few golden rules which should always be respected in order to keep your finances balanced. Before you start, calculate how long it will be before your new venture starts turning a profit. Changing career shows great initiative, but do not forget to consider the practical side of things: training, business funds, miscellaneous costs, etc. These figures often add up very quickly – do not forget that you will still have to eat!

Before you do anything else, consult your local public employment agency, as it will have information about any possible grants and financial aid that you may qualify for, which would help to cover some of the costs of your training. If you cannot rely on outside help or use your own savings, then consider temporarily staying at your current job and taking up evening or correspondence courses.

WHAT PITFALLS SHOULD BE AVOIDED?

- Do not let stress get the better of you if everything does not immediately go the way you hoped. Be patient and set yourself goals with clear deadlines. The goal is to give your professional life a boost, not to plunge you into financial and emotional ruin.

- If your plan is to effect a gradual career change involving a transitional position, do not get bogged down in your temporary situation, as this will destroy your enthusiasm and your motivation. This is another reason why planning is essential.

- Do not play games with your career. The stakes are too high, and changing career carries a lot of risks. If you find an aspect of your new job difficult, do not hesitate to apply for training or seek professional advice – all help is valuable.

- Always have a back-up plan. Be creative, as solutions can come in all shapes and sizes. For a stress-free career change, be open to other options if your first attempts are fruitless. "All roads lead to Rome", as the saying goes, and there are many ways to achieve any goal. Of course, some routes are bumpier than others, but the important thing is the destination.

OVER TO YOU:
FIVE KEY STEPS

Draw up your own action plan using the diagram below. Fill in each consecutive section to produce a summary of your ideas, and then you will be ready for action!

1. SITUATION
I want to change career.

2. ANALYSIS
Why? Lay out your motives. Is this a spur of the moment decision or are your reasons well-founded?

3. ACTION
Choose your new job. Do you already know the exact direction you want to go in? If not, do you have a sector in mind? Are you planning to draw up an overview?

4. PLAN
Draw up a plan. Investigate potential training courses, etc.

5. GO!
You are ready to aim for the stars, but do not forget that achieving your goals requires patience!

© 50MINUTES.com

We want to hear from you!
Leave a comment on your online library
and share your favourite books on social media!

FURTHER READING

BIBLIOGRAPHY

- Actiris. (2010) *Comment aborder le marché du travail.* [Online]. [Accessed 16 October 2017]. Available from: <http://www.actirisinternational. be/documents/FRANCE%20-%20FRANCE%20 -%20FRANKRIJK/Comment%20aborder%20 le%20march%C3%A9%20du%20travail%20(fr). pdf>

- Dutheil, C. and Losada, M. (2012) Quête de sens au travail : des métiers en mutation. *L'Express.* [Online]. [Accessed 16 October 2017]. Available from: <http://www.lexpress.fr/emploi/business- et-sens/quete-de-sens-au-travail-des-metiers-en- mutation_1165238.html>

- Franken, P. (2010) Suis-je bon pour une recon- version ? *Je me reconvertis.* [Online]. [Accessed 16 October 2017]. Available from: <http://www. jemereconvertis.fr/index.php?id=408>

- Gellé, E. (2014) Ressources humaines : les 5 grandes tendances de 2015. *Les Échos.* [Online]. [Accessed 16 October 2017]. Available from: <http:// archives.lesechos.fr/archives/cercle/2014/12/21/ cercle_120330.htm>

- Hohmann, C. (2014) La pyramide de Maslow.

Christian Hohmann. [Online]. [Accessed 16 October 2017]. Available from: <http://christian.hohmann.free.fr/index.php/management-du-changement/348-la-pyramide-de-maslow>

- Mazelin Salvi, F. (2013) 4 exercices pour identifier vos priorités. *Psychologies*. [Online]. [Accessed 16 October 2017]. Available from: <http://www.psychologies.com/Moi/Se-connaitre/Comportement/Articles-et-Dossiers/Aller-a-l-essentiel/4-exercices-pour-identifier-vos-priorites>

- Psychologue du travail. (2009) *La pyramide des besoins de Maslow*. [Online]. [Accessed 16 October 2017]. Available from: <http://www.psychologuedutravail.com/psychologie-du-travail/la-pyramide-des-besoins-de-maslow>

- Respect au travail. (No date) *Les risques psychosociaux*. [Online]. [Accessed 16 October 2017]. Available from: <http://respectautravail.be>

- RSE Magazine. (2013) *Comment surmonter la perte de sens au travail?* [Online]. [Accessed 16 October 2017]. Available from: <http://www.rse-magazine.com/Comment-surmonter-la-perte-de-sens-au-travail_a252.html>

ADDITIONAL SOURCES

- Charlier, M. (2017) *Developing Your Career Strategy*. Trans. Neal, R. Brussels: Plurilingua Publishing.

- Pile, T. and Lingle, D. (2016) *Changing Careers After 40: Real Stories, New Callings*. Lake Forest Park: Third Place Press.

Although the editor makes every effort to verify the accuracy of the information published, 50Minutes. com accepts no responsibility for the content of this book.

www.50minutes.com

Ebook EAN: 9782808000437

Paperback EAN: 9782808000444

Legal Deposit: D/2017/12603/449

Cover: © Primento

Digital conception by Primento, the digital partner of publishers.

Printed in Great Britain
by Amazon